a way of hope

seven steps toward breaking the cycle of violence

by Leslie J. Barner

A Way of Hope: Seven Steps toward Breaking the Cycle of Violence in Your Life

FamilyLife Publishing®
5800 Ranch Drive
Little Rock, Arkansas 72223
1-800-FL-TODAY · FamilyLife.com

FLTI, d/b/a FamilyLife®, is a ministry of Campus Crusade for Christ International®

ISBN 978-1-60200-467-2

Written and compiled by Leslie J. Barner

Printed in the United States of America

Second Edition

This resource contains material quoted from and adapted from resources developed by people who have experience and expertise in the area of domestic violence. However, quoting from these materials does not mean we endorse those materials in their entirety.

19 18 17 16 15   1 2 3 4 5

FAMILYLIFE®

contents

a word from FamilyLife

Each year, millions of women are abused in the one place they thought they would be safe: their homes. We have created this resource for two purposes:

- To give abused women hope that their lives can change
- To provide some suggestions for how to move toward recovery

This is not a comprehensive study or complete guide on domestic violence. And it doesn't provide all the necessary answers and help you will need. Our aim is to help you understand what is going on in your relationship, give you some insight into what domestic violence is about, and provide you with some guidance on how to change and rebuild your life and marriage.

Some of you also may be reading this booklet because you know someone in an abusive situation and you want to help. This material will give you important information that would help you be a supportive friend during this difficult time. It is our hope that you will gain understanding about what is happening to your friend and what domestic violence and battering is all about. You may then want to pass this booklet on to your friend or walk through the material with her step by step.

For the sake of simplicity, we have chosen to use the word "husband" when referring to the abuser. We realize many victims of abuse are single and that a growing number of men are abused by their wives. Please read through the material knowing that you may need to adapt it to your specific circumstances.

Our prayer is that this book will be for you a way of hope.

step one

Recognize the need for change

sara's story

The following is a true story, but details have been changed to protect the woman who tells it.

I was seventeen years old and about to enter my senior year of high school. I met Kurt, a terrific guy who thought I was "perfect," and we started dating. I thought I was in love.

Kurt lived a couple of hours away, so it was a long-distance relationship. (I'm sure my parents were thankful.) We talked on the phone every Wednesday for an hour or so. Some weekends my parents would allow him to stay at our house with strict rules enforced. I was always very obedient and knew not to step out of line.

My first indication that he had a temper was during a phone conversation one Wednesday. Kurt and his dad had just had a fight, and he told me he had put his fist through his bedroom wall. When I told my mom about this, her comment was, “If he's hitting walls today, he might be hitting you tomorrow.” I told her he would never do that because he loved me too much.

We were married three weeks after my high school graduation. My parents were devastated that I was not attending college; it had been their dream and mine for years. I had never had any real confidence in my abilities and practically no self-esteem. So I decided to take the easy way out.

Soon I noticed that my new husband was extremely jealous and protective. He accused me of sleeping with his friends. He would not allow me to visit my family; he seemed to feel threatened when anyone took attention away from him. When my parents would come into town to visit, he wouldn't allow me to go shopping with my mom or spend time with them. He didn't allow me to go anywhere without him, and only he could drive our vehicle.

Even worse, I was becoming afraid of him. He had begun to fly into rages for no apparent reason. Up to this point, the worst that had happened were horrible arguments and lots of tears. Every outburst was followed by flowers and apologies that he wouldn't do it again.

Then I found out I was pregnant. Kurt seemed so happy and anxious. Then within a few months it seemed that all hell broke loose. It started one day as we were driving. He said this child couldn't be his, that he knew I had been with someone else, then he began screaming and calling me names. Then his fist seemed to come out of nowhere—hitting me in the stomach! I remember grabbing my stomach, doubling over and moaning out loud. I was terrified that he had hurt the baby, and I really couldn't believe what had just happened.

Kurt immediately pulled off the road and tried to hug me as his tears flowed. He kept asking me to forgive him, and he promised it would never happen again. I was hurting so badly, I just wanted to die.

He kept his word for a few weeks. But then he flew into a rage one night and began throwing things and breaking anything in his path. This continued off and on until our son was born. Then life truly became a living hell.

The rages were even more frequent; now Kurt was convinced that I was sleeping with my coworkers. Nothing I said could convince him that I wasn't. The physical abuse really began at this point. I tried to cover the bruises with makeup or with long sleeves. I was so afraid my coworkers would find out, and I couldn't bear the embarrassment.

Kurt began calling me at work to "check up on me." Then he started missing work and sitting in the adjoining parking lot so he could watch my office building. I felt alone and confused. I wanted to tell my parents, but I was afraid they wouldn't understand.

One night we went to the store and were bringing in groceries when something set him off. I was bringing in our son from the car when Kurt attacked me and shoved me down the stairs. I lost my balance and fell backward with Michael in my arms. I was trying to hold onto him with one arm and trying to stop us with the other. Finally, about halfway down, we landed, and blood was everywhere. By the grace of God, only the arm of our son was scratched, but my leg and knee were gashed.

I told Kurt that I would kill him if he ever laid another hand on me when our son was nearby. Kurt began crying, apologizing, and begging me to forgive him. I was repulsed by what I saw in him and what I saw in myself. I remember crying out to God and asking Him to protect me and my son.

you are not alone

Perhaps you can relate in some ways to Sara's experience.

When you are abused, you feel desperately alone. You may think, "Why me? Other women don't have this problem. Something must be wrong with me." And you may feel so ashamed that this is happening to you that you don't want anyone to know about it. But the truth is that many wives suffer some form of domestic abuse, regardless of racial, religious, educational, or economic backgrounds.

According to the American Medical Association, as many as 1.9 million women around the world are physically assaulted every year. Some type of abuse from a male partner is reported by 10 to 50 percent of women.[1]

Many of these women feel trapped, anxious, afraid, and helpless. Some feel they are to blame—that if they could just do better at pleasing their husbands, they could change their situations. Others don't know what to do or where to go to get help. Most suffer in silence, hiding their situations from family and friends because of the shame and embarrassment they feel. Or perhaps they fear others will not believe them.

No, you are not alone. And there is hope! Many women have taken bold and courageous steps to seek help, to find freedom from abuse, and to begin the journey toward a new life. Some have even seen their abusers find the help they desperately needed to stop their destructive behavior and to experience healing and recovery in their own lives. Some couples, through the help of intervention and a structured recovery process guided by pastors or qualified counselors, have been able to experience healing and reconciliation in their marriages.

Yes, it's true that change does take time, a lot of courage, and a great deal of support. But change can happen. And if you are in an abusive situation, change must happen.

what is abuse?

A crucial first step in this process will be to acknowledge and understand the abuse occurring in your marriage. Abuse means to seriously mistreat or misuse someone in order to control or overpower them. People abuse others to dominate or to prevent them from making free choices.

There are several different forms of abuse.

Emotional or psychological abuse: Mistreating and controlling someone through fear, manipulation, intimidation, and attacking that person's sense of self-worth. The abuser seeks to make his wife feel afraid, helpless, confused, and worthless. This form of abuse includes name calling, mocking, belittling, accusing, blaming, yelling, swearing, harassing, demanding isolation from family and friends, misusing authority, withholding emotional support and affection, and betraying trust.

Physical abuse: Assaulting, threatening, or restraining a person through force. Men who batter often use physical violence to control women—to scare them into doing whatever they want them to do. Physical abuse includes: hitting, slapping, punching, beating, grabbing, shoving, biting, kicking, pulling hair, burning, using or threatening the use of weapons, blocking the exit from a room or building during an argument, driving recklessly, or intimidating with threatening gestures.

Sexual abuse: Behavior that dominates or controls someone through sexual acts, demands, or insults.

This includes making someone perform sexual acts against her will, when she is sick, or when it is painful; using force (including rape in or out of marriage), threats, or coercion to obtain sex or perform sexual acts; forcing unprotected sex or sex with others; treating a person like a sex object, and name calling, using disparaging words like *frigid* or *whore*.

the cycle of violence

In abusive relationships, violence usually occurs in cycles.

1. The cycle of violence begins with increased tension, anger, blaming, and arguing.
2. Then the cycle progresses to the violent stage where the abuser begins to inflict physical violence such as hitting, kicking, and slapping.
3. After the storm of violence blows over, he may experience remorse and swear he will never resort to such behavior again. This is called the calm stage or honeymoon stage. This stage of the cycle may decrease over time.

There are several tactics a man might use to sweet talk his way back into his victim's life—or convince her to return to the home if she has left. These include showering her with love and gifts, telling her he will be a great dad, starting to attend church services, halting his drinking or other substance abuse, and starting to receive outside counseling. Often the cycle begins again, however, and continues under his control until the battered woman learns to break free.

why men batter

Abusive men come from all racial, religious, educational, and economic backgrounds. Some batterers dress in business attire, earn sizable incomes, and live in upper-class neighborhoods, while others are blue-collar workers, and still others are poor and unemployed. Many may be respected by their peers, their churches, and their coworkers.

The reasons and dynamics for abusive behavior are complex. A number of abusive men grew up in abusive homes. They were beaten as children, or they witnessed their fathers abusing their mothers. Because a man grew up in an abusive home, he may view his abusive behavior as normal. Debi Pryde and Robert Needham explain in their book *A Biblical Perspective of What to Do When You Are Abused by Your Husband*:

> Abusive behavior is learned as a young boy watches the way his father treats his mother, and makes a series of choices as to whether he approves or disapproves of this behavior. It is learned as he listens to his father rationalizing and comes to believe that the father's excuses and justifications for the abuse are legitimate. As a son craves the love and approval of his father and determines to act in a way that will win his father's acceptance or mark him as a man in his father's eyes, he is tempted to imitate his dad. . . . It is learned as he sees his father place a burden of guilt upon others without a biblical understanding of God's gracious provisions and mercy for sin. Anger is a

habit easily learned.[2]

It is important to note that some men who are abusive were never abused as children, and some men from abusive family backgrounds are never abusive toward anyone.

There are many reasons men batter, but ultimately these reasons point to a problem we all have within us. If you've raised a child, you know that you don't have to teach children to lie, take from others, disobey, or be disrespectful. We have to teach our children the opposite: how to be good. The desires within us are naturally selfish and unloving. In the Bible this desire to go our own errant ways is known as *sin*.

The Bible makes it clear that we live in a world heavily affected by sin, and that all of us are prideful, self-centered, and rebellious toward God. As Romans 3:23 says, "For all have sinned and fall short of the glory of God." Each person expresses his rebellion against God in different ways. But in the end, true and lasting change—within you and within your abuser—will not happen apart from allowing Christ to be the master, the Lord, of your lives. (For more information, see Appendix 1.)

Counselors David Powlison, Paul David Tripp, and Edward T. Welch elaborate on the profile of an abuser in their booklet *Domestic Abuse: How to Help*.[3] They note these chief characteristics of abusers:

- Pervasive selfishness underneath the violent act
- Intricate, subtle patterns of self-deception
- Intricate patterns of winsome deceit toward others
- Self-deceived versions of "confession and repentance"
- Intimidation and manipulation of their victims

Whatever his profile may be, or whatever his reasons are for battering, the abusive man needs to know that with every blow, with every harsh and abusive word, and with every effort to control, he is systematically stripping another person of her dignity as a child of God.

why women stay in abusive relationships

Women do not stay in abusive relationships because they like being abused. Nor is it true that only weak, helpless women are caught in abusive relationships. Many women who are involved in abusive relationships are strong, capable women who over time have been weakened by domestic abuse. In fact, it is often the strongest women who will stay the longest because they are determined not to give up. They remain convinced that they can change or fix their relationship. Attorney Dawn Bradley Berry writes, "A woman living with a batterer is caught up in a very complex relationship that can trap her emotionally."[4]

Many women in this emotional trap feel helpless. They simply do not believe there is any way out. And they don't believe anyone can help them . . . so they give up.

A woman might stay with an abusive husband for a wide variety of reasons she views as compelling. For example,

- She still loves him.
- She feels sorry for him and believes she can help him.
- He promises to get help.
- She feels the good times outweigh the bad.
- She believes if she can work harder to please him, he will

treat her better.

- She blames herself and thinks she deserves the beatings.
- She doesn't believe she can escape her batterer's domination.
- She may think other people will believe it's her fault.
- Her abuser threatens to kill her, others, and/or himself if she leaves him.
- She feels she cannot financially support herself and her children.
- She has no other support system available (friends, family, and so forth).
- She believes that if she stays with him, things will change and get better.
- She fears being alone.
- She came from an abusive home, so to a degree she expects the violence.
- She denies or minimizes the abuse, telling herself, for example, "It really wasn't that bad. He only hits me every few months."
- She stays because of religious or cultural beliefs.
- She believes leaving will mean she is a failure as a wife and mother.
- She does not know her legal rights and feels she has no options.
- She stays because of the children.
- She doesn't know anywhere she can move.
- She is too afraid or feels too powerless to leave.

- He isn't always brutal; he can be very loving when he's not abusive.
- She is unaware of the resources available to her.[5]

Many of these reasons revolve around a core sense of paralyzing fear.

the effects on children

If you have children, you have another very important reason for change. Studies show that one-third of the children who witness the battering of their mothers demonstrate significant behavioral and/or emotional problems. These children may experience such problems as depression, anger and hostility, isolation, school problems (low achievement), drug or alcohol use, and more. They may attempt to receive attention through violent behavior, such as lashing out or treating pets cruelly, or by threatening their siblings or mother with violence.

Boys who witness their fathers' abuse of their mothers are more likely to inflict severe violence when they become adults. Data suggest that girls who witness maternal abuse are more likely to tolerate abuse as adults. Children from abusive homes often experience problems in their adult relationships and marriages—carrying the cycle to yet another generation.

facing the facts and facing your fears

Denying the abuse or the impact of abuse may have helped you to cope with the problem until now. However, denial is also the very thing that will hinder you from breaking the cycle of violence in your life. Denial keeps you from experiencing, at last, peace and freedom from abuse. The fact that you are reading this booklet is evidence that you are willing to acknowledge the abuse. You've already taken a courageous step.

Facing the fact that you are being abused or battered by your husband, and that his behavior is not normal, can stir up deep emotions—especially fear. You must acknowledge that fear in order to face and deal with the problem. In her book *Invisible Wounds: A Self-Help Guide for Women in Destructive Relationships*, Kay Douglas writes, "Unacknowledged fears play on our minds and sap our confidence until we have no energy left to deal with the problems at hand. The way out of fear is through it." She goes on to say, "As we face and feel our vulnerability, our fear may increase in intensity for a brief time. Then it begins to diminish."[6]

Authors Michael and Chuck Misja relate these heartbreaking words from a client coming to an awareness of wounds:

> I mislabeled things. I'm a master at not seeing what's obvious in front of me. I wouldn't see them as they really are because to see the truth is too painful. To see evil in my spouse is devastating because it crushes the hope that I will ever know the love I thirst for. To see the evil in me . . .[7]

Misja and Misja relate that in the Bible,

> God accurately assessed the condition of humankind. He didn't make excuses for them nor did he take responsibility for the way they chose to live their lives and relate to him.
>
> . . . Clearly God was not feeling sorry for himself, blaming others for his behaviors, whining, or having a

> pity party. . . . Decisions were made and action was taken without their ever "getting it." . . .
>
> If it is not recognized, relational sin will continue to destroy a marriage.[8]

The authors also admonish, "Your spouse is not likely to stop the threat of abuse until he or she has to answer to someone other than you."[9]

Take courage. Trust that God, who knows you and loves you intimately and far beyond your comprehension, will direct you as you trust Him. The Bible says in 2 Timothy 1:7 that God has not given His children a spirit of fear. He has given them a spirit of power, love, and self-control.

it's time to make the right choices

No matter what you have done or said, you do not deserve to be abused. You are not to blame for the abuse you have suffered.

If you are in an abusive situation, the first step toward new life and freedom is to recognize the need for a change in your life. Change can be difficult, and in some cases change can be frightening. However, in any type of abusive situation, change is absolutely necessary for your own well-being.

Remember, abuse is about power and control. You may be experiencing verbal or emotional abuse now. But if changes are not made to resolve your current situation, when your husband begins feeling as if he still does not have enough control, the abuse will likely escalate into more violent forms. According to the Metro Nashville Police Domestic Violence Division, "When abusers hit or break objects or make threats, almost 100% resort to physical battering."[10] What might be verbal abuse now could turn into physical abuse down the road. And no form of abuse is acceptable.

Contrary to what you may believe, *you are not powerless*! You are a worthwhile person, and you do not have to continue to accept the mistreatment of your abuser. You have the power to make your own choices.

personal growth exercises

1. Put a check mark next to each of the reasons on the "Why Women Stay" list that fit your situation. What are some other reasons you may be using to justify staying in your current situation? Why do you stay?
2. In the midst of the abuse and violence you have suffered, you may have wondered if God is really there or if He's even heard your prayers. Read Psalm 34. Take hope in His timeless words and trust Him to help you and deliver you.

On a separate sheet of paper, write out the verses that offer you the most hope. Then take a few moments right now and just talk to Him about how you feel. He really is there for you.

Bible memory verse

Fear not, for I am with you;
Be not dismayed, for I am your God;
I will strengthen you, I will help you,
I will uphold you with my righteous right hand. (Isaiah 41:10)

step two

Understand that healthy relationships have boundaries

It's important to understand that healthy relationships have clearly defined boundaries. Imagine how difficult it would be if there were no boundaries between your property and your neighbor's. She sunbathes at your poolside whenever she wants to. She helps herself to your water supply to nurture her lawn and garden. She drops over unannounced for dinner with her four kids. Her husband cuts down your prize roses to dig a horseshoe pit, and . . . well, you get the idea. The relationship would not be a friendly and supportive one for very long without some boundaries.

A river without boundaries is nothing more than a swamp. In the same way that a river needs boundaries, so every relationship needs boundaries to keep it from flowing out of control. Without boundaries there is no trust, no respect, no compassion, no fulfillment, no peace, and in some cases no safety.

God draws boundaries for relationships

Some people say that any boundaries in marriage are wrong and unnecessary. Yet God drew boundaries throughout the Bible in the Old and New Testaments (such as the Ten Commandments). These boundaries flow from the very nature and character of God, with the purpose of establishing and maintaining healthy relationships between God and us, as well as between people. It is both beneficial and necessary to establish healthy boundaries of acceptable behavior early in a relationship. In the case of abuse or mistreatment, boundaries should be drawn or reestablished when the first abuse occurs. If you have never had boundaries in your relationship, you may need some outside help in drawing some healthy boundaries. (Refer to Step Three.)

boundaries in marriage

Dr. Neil Anderson, founder and president emeritus of Freedom in Christ Ministries, makes it clear that "truth taken outside the boundary of God's will becomes error/falsehood."[1]

For example, if the leadership of a husband in the home is taken outside the boundary of love and self-sacrifice outlined in Ephesians 5, he becomes a dictator and a tyrant. If the submission of the wife does not include her role of being a "helper fit for him" and an "heir with [him] of the grace of life" identified in Genesis 2:18 and 1 Peter 3:7, she becomes abused and enslaved. The healthy Christian marriage is one where both the man and the woman willingly sacrifice their individual rights and give 100 percent of themselves to each other. Individually they each live for the other, and together they live for God. But when abuse is present, the boundaries of love and self-sacrifice have been crossed—that is, the two people are no longer loving and no longer sacrificing for the good of the other—making the relationship very unhealthy and contrary to the blueprint God intended for marriage. Boundaries need to be drawn or reestablished so that both spouses are giving to one another in a secure, protected relationship.

You or your spouse may have grown up in a home where there were no boundaries, and the relationship became unhealthy. It is critical not to perpetuate this problem in your own marriage and family. And if you have, don't succumb to despair. There is hope. With proper help and guidance, you can stop the cycle of abuse and establish the necessary boundaries for a healthy, loving relationship.

Here's an example of a dialogue demonstrating how you could set reasonable boundaries and speak the truth in love if you are being verbally abused. (Do not try this approach if you are being physically abused, as it may bring on more abuse.)

Husband: "You're no good."

Wife: "That's not true. What don't you think I'm good at?"

Husband: "Everything."

Wife: "How about if you give me some specifics so I can work on improving?"

Husband: "How about if you just shut up! You don't have a right to speak your mind."

Wife: "Yes, I do have a right to speak my mind as long as I'm not cutting down others."

As another example of wise boundaries, a wife might state clearly to her husband early in their relationship that if he ever hits her, she will leave him and file for legal separation until he gets help and resolves his temper. (Note that following through would be critical in establishing a meaningful boundary.) In an abusive relationship, there are a number of areas where boundaries and consequences for violating them need to be settled. Specific boundaries will be unique for you and your husband. However, if physical abuse is already taking place, you will probably need outside help for setting or reestablishing boundaries in your relationship. (See Step Three.)

accountability is critical

Establishing healthy boundaries is an important and significant step. But there must be accountability in maintaining those boundaries once they have been set. A husband and wife must help each other with direct but loving feedback when a boundary line is in danger of being crossed. And there must be consequences when a boundary line is crossed. Without consequences, your boundaries are unprotected, and they will disappear. That's exactly why countries have soldiers to protect borders as well as police and courts to enforce laws. Otherwise, boundaries are merely suggestions. Once you have established boundaries with consequences in your relationship, you must back up your words with actions. Without accountability, respect fades and dies. For further discussion on the roles of husband and wife in marriage, refer to Appendix 2.

your personal rights

To illustrate some of the areas where you might need to draw or reestablish boundaries in your relationship, Ginny NiCarthy and

Sue Davidson provide the following list of personal rights from their book *You Can Be Free: An Easy-to-Read Handbook for Abused Women.*[2] They suggest that everyone—man or woman—is entitled to these rights, which are often violated by abusive husbands.

- The right to state opinions, including unpopular ones
- The right to express feelings, even if you feel down
- The right to privacy
- The right to choose religion and lifestyle
- The right to be free from fear
- The right to have some time for yourself
- The right to spend money as you please
- The right to paid employment, at fair wages
- The right to choose your friends
- The right to emotional support from family and friends
- The right to be listened to by family and friends
- The right to decide whether or not to have sex

Obviously any one of these rights can be taken too far or twisted—outside the boundary of God's will—to justify or encourage selfish, sinful behaviors or attitudes. While you are entitled to freedom in these areas, each of your decisions should be passed through the filter of God's Word. For example, the right to privacy does not justify silence and secrets. Silence and secrets destroy intimacy, oneness, and accountability in marriage. Neither does the right to spend money as you please permit you to be a poor steward of your finances or allow you to use your family finances without the input and consensus of your husband. In fact, all of your spending and giving should be yielded to God. The intent of this freedom is to prevent tyrannical control of your spending without open and honest discussion.

In the same way, sex must never be forced—not even in marriage—but neither can it be withheld without reason. According to God's Word, we each give our bodies to our spouse, and we are not to withhold sex from our spouse except by mutual consent for a season of prayer (see 1 Corinthians 7:3–5). Within this context, each partner in the marriage has rights of his or her own, as well as obligations to the other. So, each of you must be available to the other, but you also must be able to say no at any given time. In God's view, sex is never forced. Nor is it used as a punishment or bargaining tool.

God's Word contains everything you need to know to live an abundant life (see 2 Timothy 3:16–17), so God instructs you to abide or live in His Word so that "you will know the truth, and the truth will set you free" (see John 8:31–32).

myth versus reality

In his book *Desperate Marriages*, author Gary Chapman defines four myths that can hold us captive in our relationships:

1. My environment determines my state of mind. Have you fallen into the trap that your happiness is determined by your spouse's behavior?
2. People cannot change.
3. In a desperate marriage, I have only two options—resigning myself to a life of misery or getting out. Have you allowed

yourself to become sidetracked by obsessing over the question, "How can I get out of this marriage and get on with my life?" Or, have you been sidetracked by yielding to the conclusion, "My life is miserable, but there's nothing I can do about it"? Neither of these sidetracks will lead you to the terminal of an intimate marriage.

4. Some situations are hopeless—and my situation is one of these. This myth . . . creates a defeatist attitude within you that stifles positive motivation.[3]

Then Chapman counters these myths with six realities:

1. I am responsible for my own attitude.
2. My attitude affects my actions.
3. I cannot change others, but I can influence others.
4. My emotions do not control my actions.
5. Admitting my imperfections does not mean that I am a failure.
6. Love is the most powerful weapon for good in the world. [4]

What myths are holding you captive? What realities and truths from God's Word could set you free?

personal growth exercises

1. Review John 15:12–17 and 1 John 1:5–10, taking note of the importance God places on the need for us to keep commandments or boundaries as a condition for fellowship with Him (being His friend). You might also review the Ten Commandments from God in Exodus 20:1–17. God set up

commandments (or boundaries) for our thoughts and actions to ensure healthy relationships with Him and each other.

2. Do you see the importance of boundaries in your relationship? Make a list of areas (a) where you feel your husband is violating boundaries you have established, or (b) where you need boundaries but have not yet established any.
3. Look at the list of personal rights. Which of these do you feel you have lost or need to reclaim? Are there any that you or your husband are twisting to justify your own selfish motives?
4. Do you feel that your husband is open to discussing boundaries, consequences, and accountability? If you fear further abuse from an attempt to establish clear boundaries, pray about where you can seek outside help as you read the remaining steps in this booklet.

Bible memory verse

For this is the love of God, that we keep his commandments. And his commandments are not burdensome. For everyone who has been born of God overcomes the world. And this is the victory that has overcome the world—our faith [in Jesus, the Son of God]. (1 John 5:3–4)

step three

Seek outside help and guidance

Do not try to make changes on your own. You will need help during the recovery process, and you will need help as you address the abuse in your marriage relationship. This is a great time to strengthen your support base of key relationships—your pastor, family members, friends, and others. These relationships may be estranged if your husband has isolated you from them. However, the effort to rekindle key relationships can be of great reward as these people can provide a listening ear, a place to go, financial support, and many other things in your time of need. They also can help provide safety if the situation is dangerous. (See Step Four.)

If you are not attending a Christ-centered church with a strong, biblical teaching ministry, now is the time to begin. The church can help you in several ways: love and emotional support, spiritual counseling (individual, marital, and family), food and shelter, financial support, and guidance. It is true that in the past many churches were not equipped to handle the problem of domestic abuse, perhaps because of lack of education about the problem, lack of resources, or an unwillingness to admit that abuse does exist in Christian homes. However, more and more churches are recognizing the need for this type of ministry. Search for a church that will intervene on your behalf and give you, and eventually your spouse, the proper biblical guidance to safety, healing, recovery, and reconciliation.

If that type of help is not available, the next option would be to find a Christian counselor with experience in this area. Other options would include a women's shelter, a licensed counselor, a rape crisis center, a crisis hotline, or some other service in your community that may specialize in helping women.

Caution: Many people in these agencies will have a worldview that is contrary to Christianity. If you use them as a resource, be wise about listening to and heeding all their counsel. (Read Psalm 1.)

Please Note: If you are struggling with alcohol or drug abuse, rehabilitation is a major step in your recovery process as you journey toward freedom from violence and abuse. You can contact local churches, hospitals, your personal physician, Alcoholics Anonymous, or other recovery groups for information on a rehabilitation program to help you overcome your addiction.

learn your rights

Outside friends and counselors can also help you learn the rights you have within the law to protect you and to help you as a person, as a wife, and as a mother. There are protection rights, such as restraining orders, to keep your abusive husband away. There are custody rights, property rights, rights regarding finances, and so forth. But you need to know what those rights are and how they apply to your situation, according to the laws in your country and, if in the United States, your state of residence, in order to exercise them. To learn about these rights, contact a Christian attorney or legal service, your local police department, your county bar association, your city or county prosecutor's office, a women's shelter, or a crisis hotline. Free legal services for battered women are rare, but they do exist. Call any of the places mentioned above to find out what is offered in your area.

personal growth exercises

1. Read 1 Peter 5:6–7.
2. Write a list of your worries, cares, and fears related to breaking the cycle of violence in your life. Talk to God about your list and tell Him that you are giving each one of those worries, cares, and fears to Him, trusting Him to help you overcome each one. And remember to thank Him for caring for you and for taking on the burden of your cares. As a symbol of your faith and trust in Him, proclaim to yourself that you no longer carry the burden of those cares. Then tear up your list and throw it in the trash.
3. Make a list of people in your support base. Then begin to work at strengthening those key relationships.
4. Remember, God is faithful. Hold on to the promises in His Word. Hold on to your hope in Him. Read Hebrews 10:23, 35–36.

Bible memory verse

And the LORD *will guide you continually*
and satisfy your desire in scorched places
and make your bones strong;
and you shall be like a watered garden,
like a spring of water,
 whose waters do not fail. (Isaiah 58:11)

step four

Determine your level of danger and develop a safety plan

Now that you have acknowledged the problem and realized that there is a need for change in your life, you must determine whether your safety is at risk as you attempt to exercise your right to live free of fear, violence, and intimidation.

If you have not yet suffered any physical abuse and do not believe you are at a serious risk of harm, you may be able to journey toward recovery while remaining in the same residence with your husband. Just remember that outside intervention (such as counseling) is almost always necessary for recovery and reconciliation.

If you have reason to believe that you or your children are at risk of harm, you must face that fact and take necessary steps to protect yourself and your children. Kay Douglas explains, "There is a natural tendency to downplay threats and to believe that our husband would never actually harm us. It is dangerous to hold on to this belief when his words tell us otherwise. Today's threats are often tomorrow's reality."[1]

If you fear for your safety, do not stay in an abusive situation because your husband has promised to get help. Take steps to get yourself and your children to safety first, and then encourage him to seek the help he needs. Leaving, and staying away until he gets help, may give him the motivation he needs to take such a big step in his life.

developing a safety plan

Keep in mind that if you decide to leave your home to protect yourself from physical harm, your husband may view your leaving as betrayal or rejection. He may become even more violent as a result. That is why you need to develop your safety plan with outside counsel and guidance. You may even need the help and protection of the police. Do not make your plans alone.

If you are staying in your home out of fear, or if your husband's words or behavior become more and more threatening, you need to work out an immediate safety plan. With the help of friends and counselors, you will need to plan where to keep keys, clothes, medications, and important documents; what to do with your children; where you will go if you have to leave suddenly; and much more. You may need to choose a safe, protected environment where you can be kept hidden from your husband.

For a sample of a safety plan, contact the Metro Nashville Police Department Domestic Violence Division at http://police.nashville.org/bureaus/investigative/domestic/index.asp, or call (615) 880-3000.

involving the police

In some circumstances, the only way to ensure your safety will be to call the police. This will give your husband a clear message that he has crossed the line, and that you refuse to accept his violent behavior. However, be aware that in doing so, you may incite his anger, thus escalating the problem. If he is arrested, you may be at greater risk when he is released. You will need to have a definite safety plan in place.

In *Invisible Wounds*, Kay Douglas makes the following suggestions for contacting the police:

- Keep as calm as possible. Tell the police the facts in detail. Show them any injuries you have received and let them know if there are any witnesses, including children.
- Always make sure the police make a report of the incident, even if they do not arrest your husband.
- If you want to, you can ask the police to transport you to a women's refuge or some other safe place.
- Always get the identification number and name of the police personnel involved. Keep a record of the date and time of your call, in case you need to follow up later.[2]

SPECIAL NOTE TO SINGLE WOMEN: If you are not married to your partner, you should immediately separate, cease any physical intimacy, and stop seeing each other. Do not seek to reconcile the relationship for a long period of time, if at all, and do not move back in together. There may be a time in the future when you could consider reestablishing contact, but only if your former partner accepts his responsibility, repents of his actions, and demonstrates a consistent, legitimate change in his life over a period of several years. If you ever want to consider marriage, do so only under the wise counsel and assistance of a minister, a Christian counselor, and/or the premarriage program at your local church.

personal growth exercises

1. God loves you and cares about you. He knows what you are going through and what you are feeling right now. Read Isaiah 53:2–5. Jesus is acquainted with grief and sorrow. He understands the depths of your feelings, and He fully accepts you. Put your hope and trust in Him for every detail of your life. He will not fail you. Read Philippians 4:5–7, and then write it out in your own words.
2. You may be unsure how to proceed from here. You might be wondering, "Should I leave or should I stay?" You might be asking, "What is the best way for my husband and me to get the help we need?" Read Proverbs 3:5–6. What does this say about where you should seek wisdom?
3. Contact your local church or a trusted friend and ask for recommendations for pastors, churches, or Christian programs equipped to counsel and assist people dealing with domestic violence. List those resources; then find out which would be of most help to you and make you feel comfortable. Work with them to develop your safety plan.

Bible memory verse

You are a hiding place for me;
you preserve me from trouble;
you surround me with shouts of deliverance. (Psalm 32:7)

step five

Move toward personal recovery by establishing a strong relationship with God

God loves and cares for you and desires that you experience His love, His peace, His joy, and the abundant life that only He can give. John 10:10 says, "The thief comes only to steal and kill and destroy. I came that they may have life and have it abundantly."

In Jeremiah 29:12–13 God tells us, "Then you will call upon me and come and pray to me, and I will hear you. You will seek me and find me, when you seek me with all your heart." This is a God who is interested in having a close personal relationship with us.

You may have grown up hearing about God and yet never experienced the abundant, rich relationship He promises to those who seek Him. Now may be the time to begin that relationship if you never have done so. (If you never have received Christ as your Savior and made Him Lord of your life, see Appendix 1: Knowing God Personally.)

You may know Christ but have neglected your relationship with Him. And now is when you need Him more than ever.

looking at yourself through God's eyes

Being abused by the man you love can cause many deep wounds—emotionally, spiritually, socially, and physically. Everyone has a need to be loved, respected, valued, trusted, understood, and needed. In an abusive situation, those needs are not being met, and you begin to feel worthless. If you do not feel loved or valued by others, you probably do not love yourself.

When you begin to feel worthless, you no longer care what happens to you. You begin to accept the circumstances that are causing you harm. You might be convincing yourself, "I probably deserve it anyway." Feeling worthless can lead to depression, eating disorders, attempted suicide, drug and alcohol abuse, and countless other destructive behaviors that lead you further into isolation and despair—and affect others you love. Living in an abusive relationship can strip you of your sense of self-worth, self-respect, and hope for a future. It can ultimately destroy you.

But God looks at you through different eyes. You are loved and accepted by God today . . . just as you are. In Jeremiah 31:3 God tells us, "I have loved you with an everlasting love."

When you begin to see your worth as God sees it, you view life from a totally different light. You realize that you are made in His image and that your life has unique purpose. Your life *is* worth living to the fullest. You begin to realize God has given you strengths, talents, and abilities to use in His service. You feel confident and secure about who you are apart from anyone else, and you don't have to worry about what others think.

step five

Rebuilding an understanding of your value to God is a very important step as you move toward freedom and recovery. It will help give you the courage and motivation you may need to make the necessary changes in your life and relationships. It will help give you the strength to take a stand and say to your abuser, "No more! I am a worthwhile person, valued and loved by God. He does not want me to be treated this way."

How do we know this is true? Look at the following scriptures as proof of God's unmatched love for you:

He created you in His image. Genesis 1:27, 31
So God created man in his own image, in the image of God he created him; male and female he created them. . . . And God saw everything that he had made, and behold, it was very good.

He loves you. 1 John 4:9–10 (TLB)
God showed how much he loved us by sending his only Son into this wicked world to bring to us eternal life through his death. In this act we see what real love is: it is not our love for God, but his love for us.

He sacrificed for you. John 3:16
For God so loved the world, that he gave his only Son, that whoever believes in him should not perish but have eternal life.

He chose you. Ephesians 1:4–5 (TLB)
Long ago, even before he made the world, God chose us to be his very own, through what Christ would do for us; he decided then to make us holy in his eyes, without a single fault—we who stand before him covered with his love. His unchanging plan has always been to adopt us into his own family by

sending Jesus Christ to die for us. And he did this because he wanted to!

He accepts you. Romans 5:8
But God shows his love for us in that while we were still sinners, Christ died for us.

He has a purpose for you. Jeremiah 29:11 (TLB)
"For I know the plans I have for you," says the Lord. "They are plans for good and not for evil, to give you a future and a hope."

He wants to meet your needs. Philippians 4:6–7
Do not be anxious about anything, but in everything by prayer and supplication with thanksgiving let your requests be made known to God. And the peace of God, which surpasses all understanding, will guard your hearts and your minds in Christ Jesus.

Everything you need is found in Him. Colossians 2:10
And you have been filled in him, who is the head of all rule and authority.

He cares about you and what troubles you. Psalm 55:22
Cast your burden on the LORD, and he will sustain you.

He promises to never let you down. Hebrews 13:5
"I will never leave you nor forsake you."

He thinks of you constantly. Psalm 139:17–18 (TLB)
How precious it is, Lord, to realize that you are thinking about me constantly! I can't even count how many times a day your

> thoughts turn toward me. And when I waken in the morning, you are still thinking of me!

When you learn to see yourself through God's eyes, you will recognize your unique beauty and value, and you will feel God's awesome and unconditional love toward you. No matter what anyone thinks, or how anyone criticizes you, always remember that the God of all creation loves you and thinks you are special!

Knowing this can inspire and encourage you to reach out to others for assistance in overcoming not only the abuse by your husband, but also any self-destructive behaviors (such as depression, eating disorders, or drug and alcohol abuse) you may have resorted to in the midst of your pain. For further help in seeing yourself through God's eyes or understanding struggles in life, refer to the recommended reading in Appendix 3.

where was God?

As you read through the last few paragraphs you may have wondered, "Where was God when I was going through all of this? Why did He allow this to happen to me?"

Counselors Powlison, Tripp, and Welch write these powerful words:

> Suffering is always a time for God's people to know and rely on the God who truly hears.
>
> God does not forget (see Psalm 10; 56:4). . . . On the contrary! God is on the move in response to our prayers for deliverance. We cannot always see this deliverance immediately, but God will . . . deliver his people. The story of God's work in the lives of those who suffer is not over.

> Jesus knows our sufferings. Jesus experienced violence at the hands of his own people. . . . In the throne room of God, [an abused woman] will be embraced by One who understands perfectly, grieves deeply, and loves completely.
>
> The cross is the timeless evidence of God's love for his people and his "toughness" with sin. Sin and suffering will always remain a mystery. . . . Yet God's love, demonstrated to us in Jesus, also exceeds the limits of our imagination and his justice leaves observers silenced.[1]

power in Christ

Remember that Satan, your enemy, wants to steal your joy and your peace. He wants to destroy your hope, your marriage, your children . . . your life. In Christ, you have power over the enemy.

James 4:7 says, "Submit yourselves therefore to God. Resist the devil, and he will flee from you." To resist the devil, you must first acknowledge that there is a problem. See your abuse for what it is. Then take a stand in the power of Christ and say to yourself, "I will accept this no longer!" Submit yourself to God: give Him your problems, your worries, your cares, and your fears (James 4:7), and allow Him to lead and guide your life (see Proverbs 3:5–6). He will be with you every step of the way toward freedom and recovery. He promises in Hebrews 13:5, "I will never leave you nor forsake you."

personal growth exercises

1. In 2 Corinthians 10:5 the Bible tells us to "take every thought captive to obey Christ." Just as an airport has a metal detector

to screen out danger, we need a thought detector to screen out thoughts about our lives that are contrary to what God thinks. How can we screen our thoughts? (Read all of 2 Corinthians 10:5 for ideas.)

2. Practice taking every thought captive to the obedience of Christ for the next seven days by counteracting untrue thoughts with truthful thoughts, such as a promise from God's Word.

   - If you are thinking, "I hate the way I look," read aloud Psalm 139:14: "I am fearfully and wonderfully made."
   - If you are thinking, "I can't do anything right," recite Philippians 4:13: "I can do all things through him who strengthens me."
   - If you are experiencing guilt as a result of sin, confess your sin, ask God for forgiveness, then read Psalm 103:12: "As far as the east is from the west, so far does he remove our transgressions from us."
   - If you are thinking that you are all alone and that God has abandoned you, recite Hebrews 13:5: "for he has said, 'I will never leave you nor forsake you.'"
   - If you are fearful about the future, remember Psalm 18:2: "The Lord is my rock and my fortress and my deliverer, my God, my rock, in whom I take refuge, my shield, and the horn of my salvation, my stronghold."

3. Read through the following ways to strengthen your identity in Christ and highlight exercises you can complete in the next couple of weeks.

   - Don't dwell on your perceived weaknesses. Instead, develop your God-created strengths. Avoid giving yourself negative labels ("I am ugly," "I am good for nothing," for example).

- See your mistakes as opportunities to learn, grow, and improve. When you sin, confess it to God (1 John 1:9), ask for His forgiveness, and embrace His love (Romans 8:1).
- Graciously accept compliments and praise and learn to compliment and encourage others.
- Choose the right kind of friends: those who will build you up, support you, and love you for who you are.
- Do not compare yourself with others (see Galatians 1:10). Enjoy your God-given uniqueness.
- Learn to enjoy life and see the humor in it. Treat yourself to activities you really enjoy from time to time.
- Take care of yourself. Take proper rest, maintain a healthy diet, and get some exercise! Strive to look your best (hair, nails, dress, and so forth)—not for the approval or attention of others, but to help you feel good about yourself.
- Focus on those areas in which God created you to excel! Remember that He made you in His image, and He loves you.

Bible memory verse

Finally, brothers, whatever is true, whatever is honorable, whatever is just, whatever is pure, whatever is lovely, whatever is commendable, if there is any excellence, if there is anything worthy of praise, think about these things. (Philippians 4:8)

step six

Encourage your husband to get help

Many batterers will not recognize or admit that they have a problem. To change, they must first recognize the behavior, admit it, and truly desire to change.

Do not try to confront your husband when the climate between you is still too hot. You may only fuel the flames, resulting in more anger, threats, and violence. Confront him and discuss outside intervention with him only when you are safe, when things are calm, and during a period when he is truly repentant and remorseful. Most important, confront your husband with the aid of those who are helping you deal with this crisis. (See Step Two.)

Initially, you would be wise to seek the prayers and advice of your pastor. He should be able to help you find two or three spiritually mature men in the church to confront your husband. Perhaps one man can serve as an accountability partner to him, challenging him to be the husband and father God calls him to be, and then walking with him through the recovery process.

Also, your pastor or counselor can help you count the cost as you determine your level of safety and whether you need to involve the police or seek legal help.

the need for counseling

In many cases abusive men need to experience healing and recovery from the pain, memories, and long-term effects of an abusive childhood.

Healing from such deep wounds often requires counseling. One great method for batterers is group therapy that focuses on anger and battering. Group therapy is a good choice because the members in the group offer support to one another and hold each other accountable. Look first for a Christian program for men that focuses on anger management. A Bible-believing church, court services, and civic health programs may also have information.

Some men will require help from a professional counselor trained in dealing with domestic violence and abusive behaviors, in addition to becoming a part of group therapy. After he has dealt with his abusive behavior and is well on his way to recovery, you might look into some programs through the church that teach men how to be godly husbands and fathers. In these groups he will be able to link up with other Christian men who will stand by him in brotherhood and friendship, challenge him to biblical manhood, and hold him accountable in his daily walk with Christ.

You will be tempted to smooth over your problems and seek an easy fix. For example, just because you forgive your husband does not mean you are required to trust him. That will only come as a result of true repentance, hard work, and a guided healing process with both psychological and spiritual counsel. The Metro Nashville Police Domestic Violence Division lists three signs that his treatment may be effective:

- He accepts responsibility for his violence.
- He goes into treatment without you.
- He goes into treatment with no strings attached, that is, he will not say, "I'll go if you will come back." This is just an effort to regain control over you.[1]

Remember, change doesn't happen overnight. Apart from God changing his heart and your husband's genuine repentance, he may have a long road ahead of him that will require some hard times, a lot of work, and a great deal of courage. However, in the long run, if he perseveres and leans upon the Lord to change him, he will gain a new outlook on life, and he will learn how to exercise self-control as he interacts with you and others day to day. He will learn how to relate to women in healthy ways, and he will eventually experience freedom from a life of shame, guilt, and hopelessness.

personal growth exercises

1. On a separate sheet of paper, write a special prayer to God on behalf of your husband. What is your prayer for him?
2. Read Ezekiel 36:26–31. In this passage, we see the prophet Ezekiel delivering a message from God to the people of Judah promising restoration from their sinful condition as a result of abandoning His ways. This passage also speaks words of hope to

the abuser. In your own words, what are those words of hope?

3. The abuser must be willing to open his heart to Christ and to the redemptive work of the Holy Spirit for God to restore him from his sinful condition. Read 1 John 1:9.
4. Read 2 Corinthians 5:17. What does this verse say about what happens to a person who truly gives his life to Christ and walks in His ways?

Bible memory verse

For nothing will be impossible with God. (Luke 1:37)

step seven

Move toward reconciliation

One of the most important questions you will ask yourself as you journey toward recovery from abuse is, "Can there be hope for my marriage?" Many of your friends and family may tell you to get a divorce, that reconciliation is all but impossible.

Apart from God's transforming power and your husband's genuine repentance (change of mind and direction), change can be really slow. He will need to understand the power of the Holy Spirit and how to be filled with the Spirit so that the fruit of the Spirit—love, joy, peace, patience, kindness, goodness, faithfulness, gentleness, and self-control—is produced in his life. Although reconciliation is a long and difficult process, our God is the God of reconciliation. He can shine light on even the darkest of hearts.

It is not God's desire that anyone live in an abusive situation, subject to harm, fear, and terror, robbed of true love, peace, and joy. In many cases a wife will need to separate (perhaps for several months) from her husband to ensure her safety, recover from her ordeal, and then pursue reconciliation. Always pursue reconciliation (with healthy boundaries), even if it takes a long time. FamilyLife's *Family Manifesto* states:

> We believe God's plan for marriage is that it be a lifelong commitment between one man and one woman. We believe God hates divorce. We believe divorce brings harm to every person involved. Therefore, reconciliation of a marriage should be encouraged and divorce discouraged. We also believe that God allows for divorce in certain situations, not because He wills it, but because of the hardness of people's hearts. We believe the Bible teaches that God allows for divorce in the case of adultery and in the case where an unbelieving spouse has chosen to abandon the commitment of marriage.
>
> We believe, however, that it is God's priority that marital oneness be restored and that, through the power of the gospel of Jesus Christ, forgiveness and reconciliation be experienced. We believe that in the unfortunate cases of abuse and abandonment, God has provided protection for an abused spouse and provision for child support through the church, civil law, godly counselors, prayer, and other practical measures. We believe God can restore broken people and broken marriages by His grace, by the power of His Spirit, and by His practical truths found in the Bible.[1]

the road to recovery

Reconciliation first requires an admission from both the abuser and the abused that there is a problem and a need for change. The abuser needs to accept responsibility for his violence. Both of them need to be willing to do whatever it takes to get the help they need to make those changes.

Reconciliation requires confessing sin and the evil of abusive behavior. It requires healing from the abuse and healing from past hurts. It requires forgiveness—which in itself is a miraculous act, one that involves divine intervention—and it involves a commitment to rebuild trust over a long period of time.

Finally, reconciliation requires guidance and accountability. To restore your relationship, you need the help of your friends and of a qualified pastor or counselor.

On the road to recovery, you will deal with pain and conflict, you will make mistakes, and you will shed tears. There will be a time of stripping away wrong attitudes and wrong ways of thinking that have prevented you from truly being one with your husband. And there will be a long process of relearning and rebuilding love, trust, mutual respect, and a marriage and family that will stand the test of time, with Christ at the center.

No matter what your situation—despite the terror, violence, and abuse you have suffered in the past—Christ has broken down every wall, to give you hope and victory. He can become your peace. He can be your way of hope. May He walk with you on your journey.

personal growth exercises

1. God wants us to talk to Him and make requests of Him, and He wants us to trust Him with everything that concerns us. Read 1 Peter 3:12. What does this verse tell you about prayer?
2. Take a few moments to stop and pray about your life and your marriage: "Dear God, What is Your will for me? What is Your will for us? Where do You want me to go from here? What do I need to do in my situation? What do You want me to be? How am I to act?" Ask Him to help you to grow in personal character, strength, and wisdom. Ask Him to help you and your husband to grow closer to Him and closer to each other.
3. To clear up any lingering uncertainty about God's will for your life and marriage, take some time now to consult His Word. Read Psalm 119:9, 11, 33–34, 133, and 37:31 about the power of His Word.
4. Every time you find yourself worrying or feeling hopeless or discouraged, stop and talk to God about it. Ask Him to help you and to give you the ability to cope. For hope and perseverance while you wait on God's will to be realized in your life and marriage, make Psalm 119:81, 116 (NIV) your prayer: "My soul faints with longing for your salvation, but I have put my hope in your word. . . . Sustain me according to your promise, and I will live; do not let my hopes be dashed."

Bible memory verse

And I am sure of this, that he who began a good work in you will bring it to completion at the day of Jesus Christ. (Philippians 1:6)

notes

Step One

1. Council on Scientific Affairs, "Violence Between Intimates" (American Medical Association, Report 7 full text, 1-00), 3.
2. Debi Pryde and Robert Needham, *A Biblical Perspective of What to Do When You Are Abused by Your Husband* (Newberry Springs, CA: Iron Sharpeneth Iron Publications, 2003), 22.
3. David Powlison, Paul David Tripp, and Edward T. Welch, *Domestic Abuse: How to Help* (Phillipsburg, NJ: P & R Publishing, 2002) 12-14.
4. Dawn Berry, *The Domestic Violence Sourcebook* (Los Angeles: Lowell House, 1998), 56.
5. Adapted from Nancy A. Murphy, *God's Reconciling Love: A Pastor's Handbook on Domestic Violence* (Seattle: FaithTrust Institute, 2003), 69.
6. Kay Douglas, *Invisible Wounds: A Self-Help Guide for Women in Destructive Relationships* (Auckland, New Zealand: Penguin, 1996), 176.
7. Chuck Misja and Michael Misja, *Thriving Despite a Difficult Marriage* (Colorado Springs: Navpress, 2009), 141.
8. Ibid., 142.
9. Ibid., 155.
10. Metro Nashville Police Department, The Domestic Violence Division, http://police.nashville.org/bureaus/investigative/domestic/index.asp.

Step Two

1. Dr. Neil Anderson, lecture at Talbot Seminary, date unknown. Used by permission.
2. Ginny NiCarthy and Sue Davidson, *You Can Be Free: An Easy-to-Read Handbook for Abused Women* (Berkeley, CA: The Seal Press, 1989), 28.
3. Gary Chapman, *Desperate Marriages* (Chicago: Northfield Press, 2008), 218-9.
4. Ibid., 219-21.

Step Four

1. Douglas, *Invisible Wounds*, 145.
2. Ibid., 189.

Step Five

1. Powlison, Tripp, and Welch, *Domestic Abuse*, 4-5.

Step Six

1. Metro Nashville Police Department.

Step Seven

1. FamilyLife, *The Family Manifesto* (Little Rock, AR: FamilyLife © 1993, 2007), 5.

appendix 1

Knowing God Personally

If you want to experience life the way God designed it, then you need a relationship with Him. If you want to live as the person God intended you to be, then you need to know the God who created you.

Our problem is that because of pride, we have rejected God's authority in our lives and have chosen to go our own way. Our sin separates us from Him. Though we may try to earn God's approval and deal with our sin by working hard to become better people, we must understand that the problem of sin runs much deeper than bad habits and will take more than our best behavior to overcome. God's Word clearly tells us that we cannot close the gap between ourselves and God on our own:

> *All we like sheep have gone astray; we have turned—every one—to his own way.* (Isaiah 53:6)
>
> *There is a way that seems right to a man, but its end is the way to death.* (Proverbs 14:12)
>
> *The wages of sin is death.* (Romans 6:23)

God is holy, and we are sinful. No matter how hard we try, we cannot come up with some plan—such as living a good life or trying to do what the Bible says—and hope we can be "good enough" to earn a relationship with God.

The bottom line: Our sin separates us from God. We need a Savior.

God's invitation

Thankfully, God has provided the way to solve our dilemma. He became a man in the person of Jesus Christ. Jesus lived a holy life in perfect obedience to God and willingly died on a cross to pay the penalty for our sin. Then He proved that He is more powerful than sin or death by rising from the dead.

> *Jesus said to [Thomas], "I am the way, and the truth, and the life. No one comes to the Father except through me."* (John 14:6)
>
> *God shows his love for us in that while we were still sinners, Christ died for us.* (Romans 5:8)
>
> *The wages of sin is death, but the free gift of God is eternal life in Christ Jesus our Lord.* (Romans 6:23)
>
> *For I delivered to you as of first importance what I also received: that Christ died for our sins in accordance with the Scriptures, that he was buried, that he was raised on the third day in accordance with the Scriptures, and that he appeared to Cephas, then to the twelve. Then he appeared to more than five hundred brothers at one time.* (1 Corinthians 15:3–6)

The life, death, and resurrection of Jesus has provided the way to establish a relationship between you and God.

appendix 1

accepting God's invitation

When the Bible talks about receiving Christ, it means we acknowledge that we can't save ourselves from the penalty or the power of sin. Receiving Christ means that we repent of, or turn away from, our sin and trust Christ to forgive our sins and make us the kind of people He wants us to be. It's not enough to just intellectually acknowledge that Christ is the Son of God. As an act of the will, we must place our faith and trust in Him and surrender our lives to Him and His plan for us:

> *For by grace you have been saved through faith. And this is not your own doing; it is the gift of God, not a result of works, so that no one may boast.* (Ephesians 2:8–9)

When we accept the incredible gift God offers us, we become His children:

> *But to all who did receive him, who believed in his name, he gave the right to become children of God.* (John 1:12)

what about you?

Are things right between you and God? Is He the center of your life? Is His plan for your life the priority of your life? Or is life spinning out of control as you seek to go your own way?

If you have been going your own way, you can decide today to ask Him to forgive all your sins and begin the process of changing you. You can turn to Christ, surrender your life to Him, and begin the adventure of allowing Jesus Christ and the Scriptures to transform your life. All you need to do is talk to Him in faith and tell Him what is stirring in your mind and heart.

Prayer may be new to you, but understand that God knows your heart and is not so concerned with your words as He is with the attitude of your heart. Here is a suggested prayer to guide you:

> *Lord Jesus, I need You. Thank You for dying on the cross for my sins. I receive You as my Savior and Lord. Thank You for forgiving my sins and giving me eternal life. Make me the kind of person You want me to be. Amen.*

If you prayed this prayer, or if you still have questions about knowing God personally, please visit the website http://www.matthiasmedia.com.au/2wtl/.

appendix 2

what about the roles of husband and wife?

Some of you may hesitate to change your situation because you believe your role as a wife means you should "submit" to anything your husband tells you to do. In the same way, many husbands think their role as "head of the household" justifies their abusive behavior.

God created the institution of marriage to reflect His character. Families are key foundations of every society. He created marriage to help meet our needs for love, acceptance, and companionship. He created the family as an environment for raising godly children. And as part of His plan for marriage, God created a man and a woman with equal worth, but with differing roles and responsibilities in marriage, just as the Trinity (God the Father, Jesus the Son, and the Holy Spirit) reflects equal worth with differing roles.

Unfortunately, biblical roles are often stereotyped, attacked, and ridiculed in our culture. As a result, many husbands and wives operate according to distortions of God's original plan.

True biblical roles in marriage, however, are based upon underlying foundations of unconditional love, servanthood, and humility. God has charged each wife, for example, to fulfill the responsibilities of being her husband's "helper" (Genesis 2:18–25). Each wife is called to love, respect, and give support to her husband. She is of equal value with her husband before God and has a high and holy calling. Every wife has the responsibility to willingly and intelligently affirm, respect, and submit to her husband (Colossians 3:19) as the leader in the relationship and in his vocational choices. She is to support her husband by accepting and excelling in her responsibility as his helper.

Each husband is given the responsibility of being the servant-leader of his wife (Ephesians 5:21–29). Every husband will one day give an account before God how he has loved, served, and provided for his wife.

Nowhere does the Bible instruct a husband to dominate his wife. His responsibility is to love his wife sacrificially, and that love is characterized by taking the initiative to care for her and honor her as a gift from God. Each husband is also responsible to protect his wife and to provide for her physical, emotional, and spiritual needs. He should seek his wife's opinion and counsel, and treat her as the equal partner she is in Christ.

Ephesians 5:28–29 tells us, "Husbands should love their wives as their own bodies. . . . For no one ever hated his own flesh, but nourishes and cherishes it." Abuse is the antithesis of servant leadership.

In short, wives need to understand that nothing in Scripture allows their husbands to abuse them, and nothing in Scripture instructs them to submit to abuse.

appendix 3

recommended reading for thinking correctly about yourself and building a godly family

Note: Each item in this recommended reading list contains very helpful information, even though FamilyLife might not endorse everything in each resource. Read all books prayerfully, with an eye toward what the Scriptures teach.

thinking correctly about yourself

How Can I Be Sure I'm a Christian? by Donald S. Whitney
Victory over the Darkness by Neil T. Anderson
The Holy Spirit: The Key to Supernatural Living by Bill Bright
A Woman's Journey to the Heart of God by Cynthia Heald
Boundaries in Marriage by Henry Cloud and John Townsend

hard times

Disappointment with God by Philip Yancey
Where Is God When It Hurts? by Philip Yancey
Angry Men and the Women Who Love Them by Paul Hegstrom
Unbelieving Husbands and the Wives Who Love Them by Michael Fanstone
Choosing Wisely Before You Divorce, a video resource kit from DivorceCare
Before a Bad Goodbye by Tim Clinton

marriage

Starting Your Marriage Right by Dennis and Barbara Rainey
Moments Together for Couples by Dennis and Barbara Rainey
Dr. Rosberg's Do-It-Yourself Relationship Mender by Dr. Gary Rosberg
The New Building Your Mate's Self-Esteem by Dennis and Barbara Rainey
The Five Love Needs of Men and Women by Dr. Gary and Barbara Rosberg
Rocking the Roles by Robert Lewis and William Hendricks

men

The Christian Husband by Bob Lepine
Stepping Up by Dennis Rainey
Tender Warrior by Stu Weber
Basic Training for a Few Good Men by Tim Kimmel
Guard Your Heart by Dr. Gary and Barbara Rosberg
Every Man's Battle by Fred Stoeker and Stephen Arterburn

women

The Excellent Wife by Martha Peace
The Power of a Praying Wife by Stormie Omartian
Woman of Splendor by Linda Weber
Liberated through Submission by P.B. (Bunny) Wilson
Lies Women Believe: And the Truth That Sets Them Free by Nancy Leigh DeMoss

parenting

Shepherding Your Child's Heart by Tedd Tripp
How to Really Love Your Child by Ross Campbell, M.D.
Parenting Today's Adolescent by Dennis and Barbara Rainey
How to Really Love Your Teenager by Ross Campbell, M.D.
While They Are Sleeping: Praying Character into Your Children by Anne Arkins and Gary Harrell
Encouragement for the Broken-Hearted Parent by Leslie Barner
Kids in Danger by Ross Campbell, M.D.

To obtain helpful marriage, parenting, and family resources, visit our website **FamilyLife.com**, or call **1-800-FL-TODAY**.